Notary Information

AF679482

Name:

County/City:

Commission Number:

Commission Expiration Date:

Commissioned State:

Phone Number:

Email:

Commissioned State:

Log Book Information

Start Date:

End Date:

Introduction & Legal Disclaimer

This Notary Public Journal is designed for general use in all U.S. states. Individual state laws may vary. Notaries are responsible for understanding and complying with their own state's requirements regarding recordkeeping, entries, thumbprints, and notarization procedures.

Important Disclaimer:

This journal is intended as a general guide and does not constitute legal advice. Individual state laws, regulations, and requirements for notarial journals, recordkeeping, and procedures may vary significantly.

Notaries are solely responsible for understanding and complying with all applicable laws in their jurisdiction, including but not limited to:

- Required entries for each notarial act
- Use of thumbprints (if mandated)
- Proper identification and verification of signers
- Acceptable notarial certificates and seal use
- Retention, storage, and privacy of notary records

Consult your Secretary of State, Notary Division, or applicable governing body to ensure compliance.

Use this journal with diligence, integrity, and in full accordance with the law.

Notary Creed of Integrity

As a commissioned Notary Public, I solemnly pledge to uphold the highest standards of honesty, integrity, and impartiality in every notarial act I perform.

I will carry out my duties with truthfulness, sincerity, and unwavering commitment to ethical principles.

I will serve all individuals equally, without bias, favoritism, or discrimination, and will never notarize any document in which I have a personal interest.

I will strictly adhere to the laws and regulations governing notarial acts in my jurisdiction and stay informed of any legal changes that affect my duties.

I will take all necessary steps to verify the identity of signers and ensure that they are acting willingly and knowingly, without coercion or impairment.

I will respect the privacy of all individuals and will not disclose any information obtained in the course of my notarial duties, unless required by law.

I will maintain a complete, accurate, and secure notary journal, documenting each notarial act with care and attention to detail.

I will represent the notary office with professionalism, dignity, and a commitment to excellence in public service.

This is my duty. This is my creed.

I am a Notary Public – a trusted witness to the truth.

Signature of Notary Public: ________________________

Date: __________________

Notary Duties

Acknowledgments

An acknowledgment is a formal declaration by a signer that the signature on a document is genuine and was affixed voluntarily. This act is essential to verify the identity of the signer and protect against fraud.

- To confirm that the signer is who they claim to be.
- To verify that the signature is authentic and belongs to the signer.
- To ensure that the document was signed willingly and without coercion.

Steps to Perform an Acknowledgment:

- The signer must **personally appear** before you at the time of notarization.
- You must **positively identify** the signer using acceptable identification or personal knowledge.
- The signer must acknowledge—either verbally or through conduct—that the signature on the document is theirs and that it was made voluntarily.

Jurats, Oaths, and Affirmations

A jurat is used when a signer must swear or affirm that the contents of a document are true. This type of notarial act ensures the signer understands the legal significance of their statement.

Steps to Perform a Jurat:

- The signer must **personally appear** before you.
- The document must be signed **in your presence.**
- You must administer a **verbal oath or affirmation**, then have the signer:
- **Swear or affirm aloud** that the contents of the document are true.

Important: Administering the oath or affirmation is not optional. Failure to do so may invalidate the notarization. If the signer knowingly makes false statements, they may be subject to legal penalties for perjury.

Copy Certification

A copy certification is a notarial act in which the notary confirms that a reproduction of an original document is a full, true, and accurate copy of the original.

Steps to perform a copy certification:

- The **document custodian** (the individual in possession of the original) must present both the **original document** and its **photocopy** to the notary.
- You must examine the documents and confirm that the photocopy is a true, accurate, and complete reproduction of the original.
- The custodian must **swear or affirm aloud** that the contents of the original document are accurate and unchanged.

Signature Witnessing

A signature witnessing is a notarial act in which the notary certifies that a person personally appeared, was properly identified, and either signed the document in the notary's presence or acknowledged a prior signature.

- To verify that the **individual appearing** before the notary is who they claim to be.
- To confirm that the **signature on the document** belongs to that individual.
- To ensure the document was **signed voluntarily**, without duress or coercion.

Steps to perform signature witnessing:

- The signer must **personally appear** before you.
- You must **positively identify** the individual using acceptable identification or personal knowledge.
- The document must be **signed in your presence**, or you must **witness the signature** if it has already been affixed in your presence.

1	Date and Time of Notarization	Type of Notarization	Address Where Notarization Performed	Document Type and Date	Name And Address of Signer
1				Date of Document:	
2				Date of Document:	
3				Date of Document:	
4				Date of Document:	
5				Date of Document:	
6				Date of Document:	
7				Date of Document:	
8				Date of Document:	

Identification of Signer	Additional Information	Notary Fee	Signature of Signer	Right Thumbprint of Signer	**2**
☐ Personally known by the Notary ☐ ID Type and Number with Issue and Expiration Date ☐ Credible Witness		$	x	Top of thumb here	1
☐ Personally known by the Notary ☐ ID Type and Number with Issue and Expiration Date ☐ Credible Witness		$	x	Top of thumb here	2
☐ Personally known by the Notary ☐ ID Type and Number with Issue and Expiration Date ☐ Credible Witness		$	x	Top of thumb here	3
☐ Personally known by the Notary ☐ ID Type and Number with Issue and Expiration Date ☐ Credible Witness		$	x	Top of thumb here	4
☐ Personally known by the Notary ☐ ID Type and Number with Issue and Expiration Date ☐ Credible Witness		$	x	Top of thumb here	5
☐ Personally known by the Notary ☐ ID Type and Number with Issue and Expiration Date ☐ Credible Witness		$	x	Top of thumb here	6
☐ Personally known by the Notary ☐ ID Type and Number with Issue and Expiration Date ☐ Credible Witness		$	x	Top of thumb here	7
☐ Personally known by the Notary ☐ ID Type and Number with Issue and Expiration Date ☐ Credible Witness		$	x	Top of thumb here	8

1	Date and Time of Notarization	Type of Notarization	Address Where Notarization Performed	Document Type and Date	Name And Address of Signer
1				Date of Document:	
2				Date of Document:	
3				Date of Document:	
4				Date of Document:	
5				Date of Document:	
6				Date of Document:	
7				Date of Document:	
8				Date of Document:	

Identification of Signer	Additional Information	Notary Fee	Signature of Signer	Right Thumbprint of Signer	2
☐ Personally known by the Notary ☐ ID Type and Number with Issue and Expiration Date ☐ Credible Witness		$	x	Top of thumb here	1
☐ Personally known by the Notary ☐ ID Type and Number with Issue and Expiration Date ☐ Credible Witness		$	x	Top of thumb here	2
☐ Personally known by the Notary ☐ ID Type and Number with Issue and Expiration Date ☐ Credible Witness		$	x	Top of thumb here	3
☐ Personally known by the Notary ☐ ID Type and Number with Issue and Expiration Date ☐ Credible Witness		$	x	Top of thumb here	4
☐ Personally known by the Notary ☐ ID Type and Number with Issue and Expiration Date ☐ Credible Witness		$	x	Top of thumb here	5
☐ Personally known by the Notary ☐ ID Type and Number with Issue and Expiration Date ☐ Credible Witness		$	x	Top of thumb here	6
☐ Personally known by the Notary ☐ ID Type and Number with Issue and Expiration Date ☐ Credible Witness		$	x	Top of thumb here	7
☐ Personally known by the Notary ☐ ID Type and Number with Issue and Expiration Date ☐ Credible Witness		$	x	Top of thumb here	8

1	Date and Time of Notarization	Type of Notarization	Address Where Notarization Performed	Document Type and Date	Name And Address of Signer
1				Date of Document:	
2				Date of Document:	
3				Date of Document:	
4				Date of Document:	
5				Date of Document:	
6				Date of Document:	
7				Date of Document:	
8				Date of Document:	

Identification of Signer	Additional Information	Notary Fee	Signature of Signer	Right Thumbprint of Signer	2
☐ Personally known by the Notary ☐ ID Type and Number with Issue and Expiration Date ☐ Credible Witness		$	x	Top of thumb here	1
☐ Personally known by the Notary ☐ ID Type and Number with Issue and Expiration Date ☐ Credible Witness		$	x	Top of thumb here	2
☐ Personally known by the Notary ☐ ID Type and Number with Issue and Expiration Date ☐ Credible Witness		$	x	Top of thumb here	3
☐ Personally known by the Notary ☐ ID Type and Number with Issue and Expiration Date ☐ Credible Witness		$	x	Top of thumb here	4
☐ Personally known by the Notary ☐ ID Type and Number with Issue and Expiration Date ☐ Credible Witness		$	x	Top of thumb here	5
☐ Personally known by the Notary ☐ ID Type and Number with Issue and Expiration Date ☐ Credible Witness		$	x	Top of thumb here	6
☐ Personally known by the Notary ☐ ID Type and Number with Issue and Expiration Date ☐ Credible Witness		$	x	Top of thumb here	7
☐ Personally known by the Notary ☐ ID Type and Number with Issue and Expiration Date ☐ Credible Witness		$	x	Top of thumb here	8

1	Date and Time of Notarization	Type of Notarization	Address Where Notarization Performed	Document Type and Date	Name And Address of Signer
1				Date of Document:	
2				Date of Document:	
3				Date of Document:	
4				Date of Document:	
5				Date of Document:	
6				Date of Document:	
7				Date of Document:	
8				Date of Document:	

Identification of Signer	Additional Information	Notary Fee	Signature of Signer	Right Thumbprint of Signer	2
☐ Personally known by the Notary ☐ ID Type and Number with Issue and Expiration Date ☐ Credible Witness		$	x	Top of thumb here	1
☐ Personally known by the Notary ☐ ID Type and Number with Issue and Expiration Date ☐ Credible Witness		$	x	Top of thumb here	2
☐ Personally known by the Notary ☐ ID Type and Number with Issue and Expiration Date ☐ Credible Witness		$	x	Top of thumb here	3
☐ Personally known by the Notary ☐ ID Type and Number with Issue and Expiration Date ☐ Credible Witness		$	x	Top of thumb here	4
☐ Personally known by the Notary ☐ ID Type and Number with Issue and Expiration Date ☐ Credible Witness		$	x	Top of thumb here	5
☐ Personally known by the Notary ☐ ID Type and Number with Issue and Expiration Date ☐ Credible Witness		$	x	Top of thumb here	6
☐ Personally known by the Notary ☐ ID Type and Number with Issue and Expiration Date ☐ Credible Witness		$	x	Top of thumb here	7
☐ Personally known by the Notary ☐ ID Type and Number with Issue and Expiration Date ☐ Credible Witness		$	x	Top of thumb here	8

1	Date and Time of Notarization	Type of Notarization	Address Where Notarization Performed	Document Type and Date	Name And Address of Signer
1				Date of Document:	
2				Date of Document:	
3				Date of Document:	
4				Date of Document:	
5				Date of Document:	
6				Date of Document:	
7				Date of Document:	
8				Date of Document:	

Identification of Signer	Additional Information	Notary Fee	Signature of Signer	Right Thumbprint of Signer	2
☐ Personally known by the Notary ☐ ID Type and Number with Issue and Expiration Date ☐ Credible Witness		$	x	Top of thumb here	1
☐ Personally known by the Notary ☐ ID Type and Number with Issue and Expiration Date ☐ Credible Witness		$	x	Top of thumb here	2
☐ Personally known by the Notary ☐ ID Type and Number with Issue and Expiration Date ☐ Credible Witness		$	x	Top of thumb here	3
☐ Personally known by the Notary ☐ ID Type and Number with Issue and Expiration Date ☐ Credible Witness		$	x	Top of thumb here	4
☐ Personally known by the Notary ☐ ID Type and Number with Issue and Expiration Date ☐ Credible Witness		$	x	Top of thumb here	5
☐ Personally known by the Notary ☐ ID Type and Number with Issue and Expiration Date ☐ Credible Witness		$	x	Top of thumb here	6
☐ Personally known by the Notary ☐ ID Type and Number with Issue and Expiration Date ☐ Credible Witness		$	x	Top of thumb here	7
☐ Personally known by the Notary ☐ ID Type and Number with Issue and Expiration Date ☐ Credible Witness		$	x	Top of thumb here	8

1	Date and Time of Notarization	Type of Notarization	Address Where Notarization Performed	Document Type and Date	Name And Address of Signer
1				Date of Document:	
2				Date of Document:	
3				Date of Document:	
4				Date of Document:	
5				Date of Document:	
6				Date of Document:	
7				Date of Document:	
8				Date of Document:	

Identification of Signer	Additional Information	Notary Fee	Signature of Signer	Right Thumbprint of Signer	2
☐ Personally known by the Notary ☐ ID Type and Number with Issue and Expiration Date ☐ Credible Witness		$	x	Top of thumb here	1
☐ Personally known by the Notary ☐ ID Type and Number with Issue and Expiration Date ☐ Credible Witness		$	x	Top of thumb here	2
☐ Personally known by the Notary ☐ ID Type and Number with Issue and Expiration Date ☐ Credible Witness		$	x	Top of thumb here	3
☐ Personally known by the Notary ☐ ID Type and Number with Issue and Expiration Date ☐ Credible Witness		$	x	Top of thumb here	4
☐ Personally known by the Notary ☐ ID Type and Number with Issue and Expiration Date ☐ Credible Witness		$	x	Top of thumb here	5
☐ Personally known by the Notary ☐ ID Type and Number with Issue and Expiration Date ☐ Credible Witness		$	x	Top of thumb here	6
☐ Personally known by the Notary ☐ ID Type and Number with Issue and Expiration Date ☐ Credible Witness		$	x	Top of thumb here	7
☐ Personally known by the Notary ☐ ID Type and Number with Issue and Expiration Date ☐ Credible Witness		$	x	Top of thumb here	8

1	Date and Time of Notarization	Type of Notarization	Address Where Notarization Performed	Document Type and Date	Name And Address of Signer
1				Date of Document:	
2				Date of Document:	
3				Date of Document:	
4				Date of Document:	
5				Date of Document:	
6				Date of Document:	
7				Date of Document:	
8				Date of Document:	

Identification of Signer	Additional Information	Notary Fee	Signature of Signer	Right Thumbprint of Signer	2
☐ Personally known by the Notary ☐ ID Type and Number with Issue and Expiration Date ☐ Credible Witness		$	x	Top of thumb here	1
☐ Personally known by the Notary ☐ ID Type and Number with Issue and Expiration Date ☐ Credible Witness		$	x	Top of thumb here	2
☐ Personally known by the Notary ☐ ID Type and Number with Issue and Expiration Date ☐ Credible Witness		$	x	Top of thumb here	3
☐ Personally known by the Notary ☐ ID Type and Number with Issue and Expiration Date ☐ Credible Witness		$	x	Top of thumb here	4
☐ Personally known by the Notary ☐ ID Type and Number with Issue and Expiration Date ☐ Credible Witness		$	x	Top of thumb here	5
☐ Personally known by the Notary ☐ ID Type and Number with Issue and Expiration Date ☐ Credible Witness		$	x	Top of thumb here	6
☐ Personally known by the Notary ☐ ID Type and Number with Issue and Expiration Date ☐ Credible Witness		$	x	Top of thumb here	7
☐ Personally known by the Notary ☐ ID Type and Number with Issue and Expiration Date ☐ Credible Witness		$	x	Top of thumb here	8

1	Date and Time of Notarization	Type of Notarization	Address Where Notarization Performed	Document Type and Date	Name And Address of Signer
1				Date of Document:	
2				Date of Document:	
3				Date of Document:	
4				Date of Document:	
5				Date of Document:	
6				Date of Document:	
7				Date of Document:	
8				Date of Document:	

Identification of Signer	Additional Information	Notary Fee	Signature of Signer	Right Thumbprint of Signer	2
☐ Personally known by the Notary ☐ ID Type and Number with Issue and Expiration Date ☐ Credible Witness		$	x	Top of thumb here	1
☐ Personally known by the Notary ☐ ID Type and Number with Issue and Expiration Date ☐ Credible Witness		$	x	Top of thumb here	2
☐ Personally known by the Notary ☐ ID Type and Number with Issue and Expiration Date ☐ Credible Witness		$	x	Top of thumb here	3
☐ Personally known by the Notary ☐ ID Type and Number with Issue and Expiration Date ☐ Credible Witness		$	x	Top of thumb here	4
☐ Personally known by the Notary ☐ ID Type and Number with Issue and Expiration Date ☐ Credible Witness		$	x	Top of thumb here	5
☐ Personally known by the Notary ☐ ID Type and Number with Issue and Expiration Date ☐ Credible Witness		$	x	Top of thumb here	6
☐ Personally known by the Notary ☐ ID Type and Number with Issue and Expiration Date ☐ Credible Witness		$	x	Top of thumb here	7
☐ Personally known by the Notary ☐ ID Type and Number with Issue and Expiration Date ☐ Credible Witness		$	x	Top of thumb here	8

1	Date and Time of Notarization	Type of Notarization	Address Where Notarization Performed	Document Type and Date	Name And Address of Signer
1				Date of Document:	
2				Date of Document:	
3				Date of Document:	
4				Date of Document:	
5				Date of Document:	
6				Date of Document:	
7				Date of Document:	
8				Date of Document:	

Identification of Signer	Additional Information	Notary Fee	Signature of Signer	Right Thumbprint of Signer	2
☐ Personally known by the Notary ☐ ID Type and Number with Issue and Expiration Date ☐ Credible Witness		$	x	Top of thumb here	1
☐ Personally known by the Notary ☐ ID Type and Number with Issue and Expiration Date ☐ Credible Witness		$	x	Top of thumb here	2
☐ Personally known by the Notary ☐ ID Type and Number with Issue and Expiration Date ☐ Credible Witness		$	x	Top of thumb here	3
☐ Personally known by the Notary ☐ ID Type and Number with Issue and Expiration Date ☐ Credible Witness		$	x	Top of thumb here	4
☐ Personally known by the Notary ☐ ID Type and Number with Issue and Expiration Date ☐ Credible Witness		$	x	Top of thumb here	5
☐ Personally known by the Notary ☐ ID Type and Number with Issue and Expiration Date ☐ Credible Witness		$	x	Top of thumb here	6
☐ Personally known by the Notary ☐ ID Type and Number with Issue and Expiration Date ☐ Credible Witness		$	x	Top of thumb here	7
☐ Personally known by the Notary ☐ ID Type and Number with Issue and Expiration Date ☐ Credible Witness		$	x	Top of thumb here	8

1	Date and Time of Notarization	Type of Notarization	Address Where Notarization Performed	Document Type and Date	Name And Address of Signer
1				Date of Document:	
2				Date of Document:	
3				Date of Document:	
4				Date of Document:	
5				Date of Document:	
6				Date of Document:	
7				Date of Document:	
8				Date of Document:	

Identification of Signer	Additional Information	Notary Fee	Signature of Signer	Right Thumbprint of Signer	2
☐ Personally known by the Notary ☐ ID Type and Number with Issue and Expiration Date ☐ Credible Witness		$	x	Top of thumb here	1
☐ Personally known by the Notary ☐ ID Type and Number with Issue and Expiration Date ☐ Credible Witness		$	x	Top of thumb here	2
☐ Personally known by the Notary ☐ ID Type and Number with Issue and Expiration Date ☐ Credible Witness		$	x	Top of thumb here	3
☐ Personally known by the Notary ☐ ID Type and Number with Issue and Expiration Date ☐ Credible Witness		$	x	Top of thumb here	4
☐ Personally known by the Notary ☐ ID Type and Number with Issue and Expiration Date ☐ Credible Witness		$	x	Top of thumb here	5
☐ Personally known by the Notary ☐ ID Type and Number with Issue and Expiration Date ☐ Credible Witness		$	x	Top of thumb here	6
☐ Personally known by the Notary ☐ ID Type and Number with Issue and Expiration Date ☐ Credible Witness		$	x	Top of thumb here	7
☐ Personally known by the Notary ☐ ID Type and Number with Issue and Expiration Date ☐ Credible Witness		$	x	Top of thumb here	8

1	Date and Time of Notarization	Type of Notarization	Address Where Notarization Performed	Document Type and Date	Name And Address of Signer
1				Date of Document:	
2				Date of Document:	
3				Date of Document:	
4				Date of Document:	
5				Date of Document:	
6				Date of Document:	
7				Date of Document:	
8				Date of Document:	

Identification of Signer	Additional Information	Notary Fee	Signature of Signer	Right Thumbprint of Signer	2
☐ Personally known by the Notary ☐ ID Type and Number with Issue and Expiration Date ☐ Credible Witness		$	x	Top of thumb here	1
☐ Personally known by the Notary ☐ ID Type and Number with Issue and Expiration Date ☐ Credible Witness		$	x	Top of thumb here	2
☐ Personally known by the Notary ☐ ID Type and Number with Issue and Expiration Date ☐ Credible Witness		$	x	Top of thumb here	3
☐ Personally known by the Notary ☐ ID Type and Number with Issue and Expiration Date ☐ Credible Witness		$	x	Top of thumb here	4
☐ Personally known by the Notary ☐ ID Type and Number with Issue and Expiration Date ☐ Credible Witness		$	x	Top of thumb here	5
☐ Personally known by the Notary ☐ ID Type and Number with Issue and Expiration Date ☐ Credible Witness		$	x	Top of thumb here	6
☐ Personally known by the Notary ☐ ID Type and Number with Issue and Expiration Date ☐ Credible Witness		$	x	Top of thumb here	7
☐ Personally known by the Notary ☐ ID Type and Number with Issue and Expiration Date ☐ Credible Witness		$	x	Top of thumb here	8

1	Date and Time of Notarization	Type of Notarization	Address Where Notarization Performed	Document Type and Date	Name And Address of Signer
1				Date of Document:	
2				Date of Document:	
3				Date of Document:	
4				Date of Document:	
5				Date of Document:	
6				Date of Document:	
7				Date of Document:	
8				Date of Document:	

Identification of Signer	Additional Information	Notary Fee	Signature of Signer	Right Thumbprint of Signer	2
☐ Personally known by the Notary ☐ ID Type and Number with Issue and Expiration Date ☐ Credible Witness		$	x	Top of thumb here	1
☐ Personally known by the Notary ☐ ID Type and Number with Issue and Expiration Date ☐ Credible Witness		$	x	Top of thumb here	2
☐ Personally known by the Notary ☐ ID Type and Number with Issue and Expiration Date ☐ Credible Witness		$	x	Top of thumb here	3
☐ Personally known by the Notary ☐ ID Type and Number with Issue and Expiration Date ☐ Credible Witness		$	x	Top of thumb here	4
☐ Personally known by the Notary ☐ ID Type and Number with Issue and Expiration Date ☐ Credible Witness		$	x	Top of thumb here	5
☐ Personally known by the Notary ☐ ID Type and Number with Issue and Expiration Date ☐ Credible Witness		$	x	Top of thumb here	6
☐ Personally known by the Notary ☐ ID Type and Number with Issue and Expiration Date ☐ Credible Witness		$	x	Top of thumb here	7
☐ Personally known by the Notary ☐ ID Type and Number with Issue and Expiration Date ☐ Credible Witness		$	x	Top of thumb here	8

1	Date and Time of Notarization	Type of Notarization	Address Where Notarization Performed	Document Type and Date	Name And Address of Signer
1				Date of Document:	
2				Date of Document:	
3				Date of Document:	
4				Date of Document:	
5				Date of Document:	
6				Date of Document:	
7				Date of Document:	
8				Date of Document:	

Identification of Signer	Additional Information	Notary Fee	Signature of Signer	Right Thumbprint of Signer	2
☐ Personally known by the Notary ☐ ID Type and Number with Issue and Expiration Date ☐ Credible Witness		$	x	Top of thumb here	1
☐ Personally known by the Notary ☐ ID Type and Number with Issue and Expiration Date ☐ Credible Witness		$	x	Top of thumb here	2
☐ Personally known by the Notary ☐ ID Type and Number with Issue and Expiration Date ☐ Credible Witness		$	x	Top of thumb here	3
☐ Personally known by the Notary ☐ ID Type and Number with Issue and Expiration Date ☐ Credible Witness		$	x	Top of thumb here	4
☐ Personally known by the Notary ☐ ID Type and Number with Issue and Expiration Date ☐ Credible Witness		$	x	Top of thumb here	5
☐ Personally known by the Notary ☐ ID Type and Number with Issue and Expiration Date ☐ Credible Witness		$	x	Top of thumb here	6
☐ Personally known by the Notary ☐ ID Type and Number with Issue and Expiration Date ☐ Credible Witness		$	x	Top of thumb here	7
☐ Personally known by the Notary ☐ ID Type and Number with Issue and Expiration Date ☐ Credible Witness		$	x	Top of thumb here	8

1	Date and Time of Notarization	Type of Notarization	Address Where Notarization Performed	Document Type and Date	Name And Address of Signer
1				Date of Document:	
2				Date of Document:	
3				Date of Document:	
4				Date of Document:	
5				Date of Document:	
6				Date of Document:	
7				Date of Document:	
8				Date of Document:	

Identification of Signer	Additional Information	Notary Fee	Signature of Signer	Right Thumbprint of Signer	2
☐ Personally known by the Notary ☐ ID Type and Number with Issue and Expiration Date ☐ Credible Witness		$	x	Top of thumb here	1
☐ Personally known by the Notary ☐ ID Type and Number with Issue and Expiration Date ☐ Credible Witness		$	x	Top of thumb here	2
☐ Personally known by the Notary ☐ ID Type and Number with Issue and Expiration Date ☐ Credible Witness		$	x	Top of thumb here	3
☐ Personally known by the Notary ☐ ID Type and Number with Issue and Expiration Date ☐ Credible Witness		$	x	Top of thumb here	4
☐ Personally known by the Notary ☐ ID Type and Number with Issue and Expiration Date ☐ Credible Witness		$	x	Top of thumb here	5
☐ Personally known by the Notary ☐ ID Type and Number with Issue and Expiration Date ☐ Credible Witness		$	x	Top of thumb here	6
☐ Personally known by the Notary ☐ ID Type and Number with Issue and Expiration Date ☐ Credible Witness		$	x	Top of thumb here	7
☐ Personally known by the Notary ☐ ID Type and Number with Issue and Expiration Date ☐ Credible Witness		$	x	Top of thumb here	8

1	Date and Time of Notarization	Type of Notarization	Address Where Notarization Performed	Document Type and Date	Name And Address of Signer
1				Date of Document:	
2				Date of Document:	
3				Date of Document:	
4				Date of Document:	
5				Date of Document:	
6				Date of Document:	
7				Date of Document:	
8				Date of Document:	

Identification of Signer	Additional Information	Notary Fee	Signature of Signer	Right Thumbprint of Signer	2
☐ Personally known by the Notary ☐ ID Type and Number with Issue and Expiration Date ☐ Credible Witness		$	x	Top of thumb here	1
☐ Personally known by the Notary ☐ ID Type and Number with Issue and Expiration Date ☐ Credible Witness		$	x	Top of thumb here	2
☐ Personally known by the Notary ☐ ID Type and Number with Issue and Expiration Date ☐ Credible Witness		$	x	Top of thumb here	3
☐ Personally known by the Notary ☐ ID Type and Number with Issue and Expiration Date ☐ Credible Witness		$	x	Top of thumb here	4
☐ Personally known by the Notary ☐ ID Type and Number with Issue and Expiration Date ☐ Credible Witness		$	x	Top of thumb here	5
☐ Personally known by the Notary ☐ ID Type and Number with Issue and Expiration Date ☐ Credible Witness		$	x	Top of thumb here	6
☐ Personally known by the Notary ☐ ID Type and Number with Issue and Expiration Date ☐ Credible Witness		$	x	Top of thumb here	7
☐ Personally known by the Notary ☐ ID Type and Number with Issue and Expiration Date ☐ Credible Witness		$	x	Top of thumb here	8

1	Date and Time of Notarization	Type of Notarization	Address Where Notarization Performed	Document Type and Date	Name And Address of Signer
1				Date of Document:	
2				Date of Document:	
3				Date of Document:	
4				Date of Document:	
5				Date of Document:	
6				Date of Document:	
7				Date of Document:	
8				Date of Document:	

Identification of Signer	Additional Information	Notary Fee	Signature of Signer	Right Thumbprint of Signer	2
☐ Personally known by the Notary ☐ ID Type and Number with Issue and Expiration Date ☐ Credible Witness		$	x	Top of thumb here	1
☐ Personally known by the Notary ☐ ID Type and Number with Issue and Expiration Date ☐ Credible Witness		$	x	Top of thumb here	2
☐ Personally known by the Notary ☐ ID Type and Number with Issue and Expiration Date ☐ Credible Witness		$	x	Top of thumb here	3
☐ Personally known by the Notary ☐ ID Type and Number with Issue and Expiration Date ☐ Credible Witness		$	x	Top of thumb here	4
☐ Personally known by the Notary ☐ ID Type and Number with Issue and Expiration Date ☐ Credible Witness		$	x	Top of thumb here	5
☐ Personally known by the Notary ☐ ID Type and Number with Issue and Expiration Date ☐ Credible Witness		$	x	Top of thumb here	6
☐ Personally known by the Notary ☐ ID Type and Number with Issue and Expiration Date ☐ Credible Witness		$	x	Top of thumb here	7
☐ Personally known by the Notary ☐ ID Type and Number with Issue and Expiration Date ☐ Credible Witness		$	x	Top of thumb here	8

1	Date and Time of Notarization	Type of Notarization	Address Where Notarization Performed	Document Type and Date	Name And Address of Signer
1				Date of Document:	
2				Date of Document:	
3				Date of Document:	
4				Date of Document:	
5				Date of Document:	
6				Date of Document:	
7				Date of Document:	
8				Date of Document:	

Identification of Signer	Additional Information	Notary Fee	Signature of Signer	Right Thumbprint of Signer	2
☐ Personally known by the Notary ☐ ID Type and Number with Issue and Expiration Date ☐ Credible Witness		$	x	Top of thumb here	1
☐ Personally known by the Notary ☐ ID Type and Number with Issue and Expiration Date ☐ Credible Witness		$	x	Top of thumb here	2
☐ Personally known by the Notary ☐ ID Type and Number with Issue and Expiration Date ☐ Credible Witness		$	x	Top of thumb here	3
☐ Personally known by the Notary ☐ ID Type and Number with Issue and Expiration Date ☐ Credible Witness		$	x	Top of thumb here	4
☐ Personally known by the Notary ☐ ID Type and Number with Issue and Expiration Date ☐ Credible Witness		$	x	Top of thumb here	5
☐ Personally known by the Notary ☐ ID Type and Number with Issue and Expiration Date ☐ Credible Witness		$	x	Top of thumb here	6
☐ Personally known by the Notary ☐ ID Type and Number with Issue and Expiration Date ☐ Credible Witness		$	x	Top of thumb here	7
☐ Personally known by the Notary ☐ ID Type and Number with Issue and Expiration Date ☐ Credible Witness		$	x	Top of thumb here	8

1	Date and Time of Notarization	Type of Notarization	Address Where Notarization Performed	Document Type and Date	Name And Address of Signer
1				Date of Document:	
2				Date of Document:	
3				Date of Document:	
4				Date of Document:	
5				Date of Document:	
6				Date of Document:	
7				Date of Document:	
8				Date of Document:	

Identification of Signer	Additional Information	Notary Fee	Signature of Signer	Right Thumbprint of Signer	2
☐ Personally known by the Notary ☐ ID Type and Number with Issue and Expiration Date ☐ Credible Witness		$	x	Top of thumb here	1
☐ Personally known by the Notary ☐ ID Type and Number with Issue and Expiration Date ☐ Credible Witness		$	x	Top of thumb here	2
☐ Personally known by the Notary ☐ ID Type and Number with Issue and Expiration Date ☐ Credible Witness		$	x	Top of thumb here	3
☐ Personally known by the Notary ☐ ID Type and Number with Issue and Expiration Date ☐ Credible Witness		$	x	Top of thumb here	4
☐ Personally known by the Notary ☐ ID Type and Number with Issue and Expiration Date ☐ Credible Witness		$	x	Top of thumb here	5
☐ Personally known by the Notary ☐ ID Type and Number with Issue and Expiration Date ☐ Credible Witness		$	x	Top of thumb here	6
☐ Personally known by the Notary ☐ ID Type and Number with Issue and Expiration Date ☐ Credible Witness		$	x	Top of thumb here	7
☐ Personally known by the Notary ☐ ID Type and Number with Issue and Expiration Date ☐ Credible Witness		$	x	Top of thumb here	8

1	Date and Time of Notarization	Type of Notarization	Address Where Notarization Performed	Document Type and Date	Name And Address of Signer
1				Date of Document:	
2				Date of Document:	
3				Date of Document:	
4				Date of Document:	
5				Date of Document:	
6				Date of Document:	
7				Date of Document:	
8				Date of Document:	

Identification of Signer	Additional Information	Notary Fee	Signature of Signer	Right Thumbprint of Signer	2
☐ Personally known by the Notary ☐ ID Type and Number with Issue and Expiration Date ☐ Credible Witness		$	x	Top of thumb here	1
☐ Personally known by the Notary ☐ ID Type and Number with Issue and Expiration Date ☐ Credible Witness		$	x	Top of thumb here	2
☐ Personally known by the Notary ☐ ID Type and Number with Issue and Expiration Date ☐ Credible Witness		$	x	Top of thumb here	3
☐ Personally known by the Notary ☐ ID Type and Number with Issue and Expiration Date ☐ Credible Witness		$	x	Top of thumb here	4
☐ Personally known by the Notary ☐ ID Type and Number with Issue and Expiration Date ☐ Credible Witness		$	x	Top of thumb here	5
☐ Personally known by the Notary ☐ ID Type and Number with Issue and Expiration Date ☐ Credible Witness		$	x	Top of thumb here	6
☐ Personally known by the Notary ☐ ID Type and Number with Issue and Expiration Date ☐ Credible Witness		$	x	Top of thumb here	7
☐ Personally known by the Notary ☐ ID Type and Number with Issue and Expiration Date ☐ Credible Witness		$	x	Top of thumb here	8

1	Date and Time of Notarization	Type of Notarization	Address Where Notarization Performed	Document Type and Date	Name And Address of Signer
1				Date of Document:	
2				Date of Document:	
3				Date of Document:	
4				Date of Document:	
5				Date of Document:	
6				Date of Document:	
7				Date of Document:	
8				Date of Document:	

Identification of Signer	Additional Information	Notary Fee	Signature of Signer	Right Thumbprint of Signer	2
☐ Personally known by the Notary ☐ ID Type and Number with Issue and Expiration Date ☐ Credible Witness		$	x	Top of thumb here	1
☐ Personally known by the Notary ☐ ID Type and Number with Issue and Expiration Date ☐ Credible Witness		$	x	Top of thumb here	2
☐ Personally known by the Notary ☐ ID Type and Number with Issue and Expiration Date ☐ Credible Witness		$	x	Top of thumb here	3
☐ Personally known by the Notary ☐ ID Type and Number with Issue and Expiration Date ☐ Credible Witness		$	x	Top of thumb here	4
☐ Personally known by the Notary ☐ ID Type and Number with Issue and Expiration Date ☐ Credible Witness		$	x	Top of thumb here	5
☐ Personally known by the Notary ☐ ID Type and Number with Issue and Expiration Date ☐ Credible Witness		$	x	Top of thumb here	6
☐ Personally known by the Notary ☐ ID Type and Number with Issue and Expiration Date ☐ Credible Witness		$	x	Top of thumb here	7
☐ Personally known by the Notary ☐ ID Type and Number with Issue and Expiration Date ☐ Credible Witness		$	x	Top of thumb here	8

1	Date and Time of Notarization	Type of Notarization	Address Where Notarization Performed	Document Type and Date	Name And Address of Signer
1				Date of Document:	
2				Date of Document:	
3				Date of Document:	
4				Date of Document:	
5				Date of Document:	
6				Date of Document:	
7				Date of Document:	
8				Date of Document:	

Identification of Signer	Additional Information	Notary Fee	Signature of Signer	Right Thumbprint of Signer	2
☐ Personally known by the Notary ☐ ID Type and Number with Issue and Expiration Date ☐ Credible Witness		$	x	Top of thumb here	1
☐ Personally known by the Notary ☐ ID Type and Number with Issue and Expiration Date ☐ Credible Witness		$	x	Top of thumb here	2
☐ Personally known by the Notary ☐ ID Type and Number with Issue and Expiration Date ☐ Credible Witness		$	x	Top of thumb here	3
☐ Personally known by the Notary ☐ ID Type and Number with Issue and Expiration Date ☐ Credible Witness		$	x	Top of thumb here	4
☐ Personally known by the Notary ☐ ID Type and Number with Issue and Expiration Date ☐ Credible Witness		$	x	Top of thumb here	5
☐ Personally known by the Notary ☐ ID Type and Number with Issue and Expiration Date ☐ Credible Witness		$	x	Top of thumb here	6
☐ Personally known by the Notary ☐ ID Type and Number with Issue and Expiration Date ☐ Credible Witness		$	x	Top of thumb here	7
☐ Personally known by the Notary ☐ ID Type and Number with Issue and Expiration Date ☐ Credible Witness		$	x	Top of thumb here	8

1	Date and Time of Notarization	Type of Notarization	Address Where Notarization Performed	Document Type and Date	Name And Address of Signer
1				Date of Document:	
2				Date of Document:	
3				Date of Document:	
4				Date of Document:	
5				Date of Document:	
6				Date of Document:	
7				Date of Document:	
8				Date of Document:	

Identification of Signer	Additional Information	Notary Fee	Signature of Signer	Right Thumbprint of Signer	2
☐ Personally known by the Notary ☐ ID Type and Number with Issue and Expiration Date ☐ Credible Witness		$	x	Top of thumb here	1
☐ Personally known by the Notary ☐ ID Type and Number with Issue and Expiration Date ☐ Credible Witness		$	x	Top of thumb here	2
☐ Personally known by the Notary ☐ ID Type and Number with Issue and Expiration Date ☐ Credible Witness		$	x	Top of thumb here	3
☐ Personally known by the Notary ☐ ID Type and Number with Issue and Expiration Date ☐ Credible Witness		$	x	Top of thumb here	4
☐ Personally known by the Notary ☐ ID Type and Number with Issue and Expiration Date ☐ Credible Witness		$	x	Top of thumb here	5
☐ Personally known by the Notary ☐ ID Type and Number with Issue and Expiration Date ☐ Credible Witness		$	x	Top of thumb here	6
☐ Personally known by the Notary ☐ ID Type and Number with Issue and Expiration Date ☐ Credible Witness		$	x	Top of thumb here	7
☐ Personally known by the Notary ☐ ID Type and Number with Issue and Expiration Date ☐ Credible Witness		$	x	Top of thumb here	8

1	Date and Time of Notarization	Type of Notarization	Address Where Notarization Performed	Document Type and Date	Name And Address of Signer
1				Date of Document:	
2				Date of Document:	
3				Date of Document:	
4				Date of Document:	
5				Date of Document:	
6				Date of Document:	
7				Date of Document:	
8				Date of Document:	

Identification of Signer	Additional Information	Notary Fee	Signature of Signer	Right Thumbprint of Signer	2
☐ Personally known by the Notary ☐ ID Type and Number with Issue and Expiration Date ☐ Credible Witness		$	x	Top of thumb here	1
☐ Personally known by the Notary ☐ ID Type and Number with Issue and Expiration Date ☐ Credible Witness		$	x	Top of thumb here	2
☐ Personally known by the Notary ☐ ID Type and Number with Issue and Expiration Date ☐ Credible Witness		$	x	Top of thumb here	3
☐ Personally known by the Notary ☐ ID Type and Number with Issue and Expiration Date ☐ Credible Witness		$	x	Top of thumb here	4
☐ Personally known by the Notary ☐ ID Type and Number with Issue and Expiration Date ☐ Credible Witness		$	x	Top of thumb here	5
☐ Personally known by the Notary ☐ ID Type and Number with Issue and Expiration Date ☐ Credible Witness		$	x	Top of thumb here	6
☐ Personally known by the Notary ☐ ID Type and Number with Issue and Expiration Date ☐ Credible Witness		$	x	Top of thumb here	7
☐ Personally known by the Notary ☐ ID Type and Number with Issue and Expiration Date ☐ Credible Witness		$	x	Top of thumb here	8

1	Date and Time of Notarization	Type of Notarization	Address Where Notarization Performed	Document Type and Date	Name And Address of Signer
1				Date of Document:	
2				Date of Document:	
3				Date of Document:	
4				Date of Document:	
5				Date of Document:	
6				Date of Document:	
7				Date of Document:	
8				Date of Document:	

Identification of Signer	Additional Information	Notary Fee	Signature of Signer	Right Thumbprint of Signer	2
☐ Personally known by the Notary ☐ ID Type and Number with Issue and Expiration Date ☐ Credible Witness		$	×	Top of thumb here	1
☐ Personally known by the Notary ☐ ID Type and Number with Issue and Expiration Date ☐ Credible Witness		$	×	Top of thumb here	2
☐ Personally known by the Notary ☐ ID Type and Number with Issue and Expiration Date ☐ Credible Witness		$	×	Top of thumb here	3
☐ Personally known by the Notary ☐ ID Type and Number with Issue and Expiration Date ☐ Credible Witness		$	×	Top of thumb here	4
☐ Personally known by the Notary ☐ ID Type and Number with Issue and Expiration Date ☐ Credible Witness		$	×	Top of thumb here	5
☐ Personally known by the Notary ☐ ID Type and Number with Issue and Expiration Date ☐ Credible Witness		$	×	Top of thumb here	6
☐ Personally known by the Notary ☐ ID Type and Number with Issue and Expiration Date ☐ Credible Witness		$	×	Top of thumb here	7
☐ Personally known by the Notary ☐ ID Type and Number with Issue and Expiration Date ☐ Credible Witness		$	×	Top of thumb here	8

1	Date and Time of Notarization	Type of Notarization	Address Where Notarization Performed	Document Type and Date	Name And Address of Signer
1				Date of Document:	
2				Date of Document:	
3				Date of Document:	
4				Date of Document:	
5				Date of Document:	
6				Date of Document:	
7				Date of Document:	
8				Date of Document:	

Identification of Signer	Additional Information	Notary Fee	Signature of Signer	Right Thumbprint of Signer	2
☐ Personally known by the Notary ☐ ID Type and Number with Issue and Expiration Date ☐ Credible Witness		$	x	Top of thumb here	1
☐ Personally known by the Notary ☐ ID Type and Number with Issue and Expiration Date ☐ Credible Witness		$	x	Top of thumb here	2
☐ Personally known by the Notary ☐ ID Type and Number with Issue and Expiration Date ☐ Credible Witness		$	x	Top of thumb here	3
☐ Personally known by the Notary ☐ ID Type and Number with Issue and Expiration Date ☐ Credible Witness		$	x	Top of thumb here	4
☐ Personally known by the Notary ☐ ID Type and Number with Issue and Expiration Date ☐ Credible Witness		$	x	Top of thumb here	5
☐ Personally known by the Notary ☐ ID Type and Number with Issue and Expiration Date ☐ Credible Witness		$	x	Top of thumb here	6
☐ Personally known by the Notary ☐ ID Type and Number with Issue and Expiration Date ☐ Credible Witness		$	x	Top of thumb here	7
☐ Personally known by the Notary ☐ ID Type and Number with Issue and Expiration Date ☐ Credible Witness		$	x	Top of thumb here	8

1	Date and Time of Notarization	Type of Notarization	Address Where Notarization Performed	Document Type and Date	Name And Address of Signer
1				Date of Document:	
2				Date of Document:	
3				Date of Document:	
4				Date of Document:	
5				Date of Document:	
6				Date of Document:	
7				Date of Document:	
8				Date of Document:	

Identification of Signer	Additional Information	Notary Fee	Signature of Signer	Right Thumbprint of Signer	2
☐ Personally known by the Notary ☐ ID Type and Number with Issue and Expiration Date ☐ Credible Witness		$	x	Top of thumb here	1
☐ Personally known by the Notary ☐ ID Type and Number with Issue and Expiration Date ☐ Credible Witness		$	x	Top of thumb here	2
☐ Personally known by the Notary ☐ ID Type and Number with Issue and Expiration Date ☐ Credible Witness		$	x	Top of thumb here	3
☐ Personally known by the Notary ☐ ID Type and Number with Issue and Expiration Date ☐ Credible Witness		$	x	Top of thumb here	4
☐ Personally known by the Notary ☐ ID Type and Number with Issue and Expiration Date ☐ Credible Witness		$	x	Top of thumb here	5
☐ Personally known by the Notary ☐ ID Type and Number with Issue and Expiration Date ☐ Credible Witness		$	x	Top of thumb here	6
☐ Personally known by the Notary ☐ ID Type and Number with Issue and Expiration Date ☐ Credible Witness		$	x	Top of thumb here	7
☐ Personally known by the Notary ☐ ID Type and Number with Issue and Expiration Date ☐ Credible Witness		$	x	Top of thumb here	8

1	Date and Time of Notarization	Type of Notarization	Address Where Notarization Performed	Document Type and Date	Name And Address of Signer
1				Date of Document:	
2				Date of Document:	
3				Date of Document:	
4				Date of Document:	
5				Date of Document:	
6				Date of Document:	
7				Date of Document:	
8				Date of Document:	

Identification of Signer	Additional Information	Notary Fee	Signature of Signer	Right Thumbprint of Signer	2
☐ Personally known by the Notary ☐ ID Type and Number with Issue and Expiration Date ☐ Credible Witness		$	x	Top of thumb here	1
☐ Personally known by the Notary ☐ ID Type and Number with Issue and Expiration Date ☐ Credible Witness		$	x	Top of thumb here	2
☐ Personally known by the Notary ☐ ID Type and Number with Issue and Expiration Date ☐ Credible Witness		$	x	Top of thumb here	3
☐ Personally known by the Notary ☐ ID Type and Number with Issue and Expiration Date ☐ Credible Witness		$	x	Top of thumb here	4
☐ Personally known by the Notary ☐ ID Type and Number with Issue and Expiration Date ☐ Credible Witness		$	x	Top of thumb here	5
☐ Personally known by the Notary ☐ ID Type and Number with Issue and Expiration Date ☐ Credible Witness		$	x	Top of thumb here	6
☐ Personally known by the Notary ☐ ID Type and Number with Issue and Expiration Date ☐ Credible Witness		$	x	Top of thumb here	7
☐ Personally known by the Notary ☐ ID Type and Number with Issue and Expiration Date ☐ Credible Witness		$	x	Top of thumb here	8

1	Date and Time of Notarization	Type of Notarization	Address Where Notarization Performed	Document Type and Date	Name And Address of Signer
1				Date of Document:	
2				Date of Document:	
3				Date of Document:	
4				Date of Document:	
5				Date of Document:	
6				Date of Document:	
7				Date of Document:	
8				Date of Document:	

Identification of Signer	Additional Information	Notary Fee	Signature of Signer	Right Thumbprint of Signer	2
☐ Personally known by the Notary ☐ ID Type and Number with Issue and Expiration Date ☐ Credible Witness		$	x	Top of thumb here	1
☐ Personally known by the Notary ☐ ID Type and Number with Issue and Expiration Date ☐ Credible Witness		$	x	Top of thumb here	2
☐ Personally known by the Notary ☐ ID Type and Number with Issue and Expiration Date ☐ Credible Witness		$	x	Top of thumb here	3
☐ Personally known by the Notary ☐ ID Type and Number with Issue and Expiration Date ☐ Credible Witness		$	x	Top of thumb here	4
☐ Personally known by the Notary ☐ ID Type and Number with Issue and Expiration Date ☐ Credible Witness		$	x	Top of thumb here	5
☐ Personally known by the Notary ☐ ID Type and Number with Issue and Expiration Date ☐ Credible Witness		$	x	Top of thumb here	6
☐ Personally known by the Notary ☐ ID Type and Number with Issue and Expiration Date ☐ Credible Witness		$	x	Top of thumb here	7
☐ Personally known by the Notary ☐ ID Type and Number with Issue and Expiration Date ☐ Credible Witness		$	x	Top of thumb here	8

1	Date and Time of Notarization	Type of Notarization	Address Where Notarization Performed	Document Type and Date	Name And Address of Signer
1				Date of Document:	
2				Date of Document:	
3				Date of Document:	
4				Date of Document:	
5				Date of Document:	
6				Date of Document:	
7				Date of Document:	
8				Date of Document:	

Identification of Signer	Additional Information	Notary Fee	Signature of Signer	Right Thumbprint of Signer	2
☐ Personally known by the Notary ☐ ID Type and Number with Issue and Expiration Date ☐ Credible Witness		$	x	Top of thumb here	1
☐ Personally known by the Notary ☐ ID Type and Number with Issue and Expiration Date ☐ Credible Witness		$	x	Top of thumb here	2
☐ Personally known by the Notary ☐ ID Type and Number with Issue and Expiration Date ☐ Credible Witness		$	x	Top of thumb here	3
☐ Personally known by the Notary ☐ ID Type and Number with Issue and Expiration Date ☐ Credible Witness		$	x	Top of thumb here	4
☐ Personally known by the Notary ☐ ID Type and Number with Issue and Expiration Date ☐ Credible Witness		$	x	Top of thumb here	5
☐ Personally known by the Notary ☐ ID Type and Number with Issue and Expiration Date ☐ Credible Witness		$	x	Top of thumb here	6
☐ Personally known by the Notary ☐ ID Type and Number with Issue and Expiration Date ☐ Credible Witness		$	x	Top of thumb here	7
☐ Personally known by the Notary ☐ ID Type and Number with Issue and Expiration Date ☐ Credible Witness		$	x	Top of thumb here	8

1	Date and Time of Notarization	Type of Notarization	Address Where Notarization Performed	Document Type and Date	Name And Address of Signer
1				Date of Document:	
2				Date of Document:	
3				Date of Document:	
4				Date of Document:	
5				Date of Document:	
6				Date of Document:	
7				Date of Document:	
8				Date of Document:	

Identification of Signer	Additional Information	Notary Fee	Signature of Signer	Right Thumbprint of Signer	2
☐ Personally known by the Notary ☐ ID Type and Number with Issue and Expiration Date ☐ Credible Witness		$	x	Top of thumb here	1
☐ Personally known by the Notary ☐ ID Type and Number with Issue and Expiration Date ☐ Credible Witness		$	x	Top of thumb here	2
☐ Personally known by the Notary ☐ ID Type and Number with Issue and Expiration Date ☐ Credible Witness		$	x	Top of thumb here	3
☐ Personally known by the Notary ☐ ID Type and Number with Issue and Expiration Date ☐ Credible Witness		$	x	Top of thumb here	4
☐ Personally known by the Notary ☐ ID Type and Number with Issue and Expiration Date ☐ Credible Witness		$	x	Top of thumb here	5
☐ Personally known by the Notary ☐ ID Type and Number with Issue and Expiration Date ☐ Credible Witness		$	x	Top of thumb here	6
☐ Personally known by the Notary ☐ ID Type and Number with Issue and Expiration Date ☐ Credible Witness		$	x	Top of thumb here	7
☐ Personally known by the Notary ☐ ID Type and Number with Issue and Expiration Date ☐ Credible Witness		$	x	Top of thumb here	8

1	Date and Time of Notarization	Type of Notarization	Address Where Notarization Performed	Document Type and Date	Name And Address of Signer
1				Date of Document:	
2				Date of Document:	
3				Date of Document:	
4				Date of Document:	
5				Date of Document:	
6				Date of Document:	
7				Date of Document:	
8				Date of Document:	

Identification of Signer	Additional Information	Notary Fee	Signature of Signer	Right Thumbprint of Signer	2
☐ Personally known by the Notary ☐ ID Type and Number with Issue and Expiration Date ☐ Credible Witness		$	x	Top of thumb here	1
☐ Personally known by the Notary ☐ ID Type and Number with Issue and Expiration Date ☐ Credible Witness		$	x	Top of thumb here	2
☐ Personally known by the Notary ☐ ID Type and Number with Issue and Expiration Date ☐ Credible Witness		$	x	Top of thumb here	3
☐ Personally known by the Notary ☐ ID Type and Number with Issue and Expiration Date ☐ Credible Witness		$	x	Top of thumb here	4
☐ Personally known by the Notary ☐ ID Type and Number with Issue and Expiration Date ☐ Credible Witness		$	x	Top of thumb here	5
☐ Personally known by the Notary ☐ ID Type and Number with Issue and Expiration Date ☐ Credible Witness		$	x	Top of thumb here	6
☐ Personally known by the Notary ☐ ID Type and Number with Issue and Expiration Date ☐ Credible Witness		$	x	Top of thumb here	7
☐ Personally known by the Notary ☐ ID Type and Number with Issue and Expiration Date ☐ Credible Witness		$	x	Top of thumb here	8

1	Date and Time of Notarization	Type of Notarization	Address Where Notarization Performed	Document Type and Date	Name And Address of Signer
1				Date of Document:	
2				Date of Document:	
3				Date of Document:	
4				Date of Document:	
5				Date of Document:	
6				Date of Document:	
7				Date of Document:	
8				Date of Document:	

Identification of Signer	Additional Information	Notary Fee	Signature of Signer	Right Thumbprint of Signer	2
☐ Personally known by the Notary ☐ ID Type and Number with Issue and Expiration Date ☐ Credible Witness		$	x	Top of thumb here	1
☐ Personally known by the Notary ☐ ID Type and Number with Issue and Expiration Date ☐ Credible Witness		$	x	Top of thumb here	2
☐ Personally known by the Notary ☐ ID Type and Number with Issue and Expiration Date ☐ Credible Witness		$	x	Top of thumb here	3
☐ Personally known by the Notary ☐ ID Type and Number with Issue and Expiration Date ☐ Credible Witness		$	x	Top of thumb here	4
☐ Personally known by the Notary ☐ ID Type and Number with Issue and Expiration Date ☐ Credible Witness		$	x	Top of thumb here	5
☐ Personally known by the Notary ☐ ID Type and Number with Issue and Expiration Date ☐ Credible Witness		$	x	Top of thumb here	6
☐ Personally known by the Notary ☐ ID Type and Number with Issue and Expiration Date ☐ Credible Witness		$	x	Top of thumb here	7
☐ Personally known by the Notary ☐ ID Type and Number with Issue and Expiration Date ☐ Credible Witness		$	x	Top of thumb here	8

1	Date and Time of Notarization	Type of Notarization	Address Where Notarization Performed	Document Type and Date	Name And Address of Signer
1				Date of Document:	
2				Date of Document:	
3				Date of Document:	
4				Date of Document:	
5				Date of Document:	
6				Date of Document:	
7				Date of Document:	
8				Date of Document:	

Identification of Signer	Additional Information	Notary Fee	Signature of Signer	Right Thumbprint of Signer	2
☐ Personally known by the Notary ☐ ID Type and Number with Issue and Expiration Date ☐ Credible Witness		$	x	Top of thumb here	1
☐ Personally known by the Notary ☐ ID Type and Number with Issue and Expiration Date ☐ Credible Witness		$	x	Top of thumb here	2
☐ Personally known by the Notary ☐ ID Type and Number with Issue and Expiration Date ☐ Credible Witness		$	x	Top of thumb here	3
☐ Personally known by the Notary ☐ ID Type and Number with Issue and Expiration Date ☐ Credible Witness		$	x	Top of thumb here	4
☐ Personally known by the Notary ☐ ID Type and Number with Issue and Expiration Date ☐ Credible Witness		$	x	Top of thumb here	5
☐ Personally known by the Notary ☐ ID Type and Number with Issue and Expiration Date ☐ Credible Witness		$	x	Top of thumb here	6
☐ Personally known by the Notary ☐ ID Type and Number with Issue and Expiration Date ☐ Credible Witness		$	x	Top of thumb here	7
☐ Personally known by the Notary ☐ ID Type and Number with Issue and Expiration Date ☐ Credible Witness		$	x	Top of thumb here	8

1	Date and Time of Notarization	Type of Notarization	Address Where Notarization Performed	Document Type and Date	Name And Address of Signer
1				Date of Document:	
2				Date of Document:	
3				Date of Document:	
4				Date of Document:	
5				Date of Document:	
6				Date of Document:	
7				Date of Document:	
8				Date of Document:	

Identification of Signer	Additional Information	Notary Fee	Signature of Signer	Right Thumbprint of Signer	2
☐ Personally known by the Notary ☐ ID Type and Number with Issue and Expiration Date ☐ Credible Witness		$	x	Top of thumb here	1
☐ Personally known by the Notary ☐ ID Type and Number with Issue and Expiration Date ☐ Credible Witness		$	x	Top of thumb here	2
☐ Personally known by the Notary ☐ ID Type and Number with Issue and Expiration Date ☐ Credible Witness		$	x	Top of thumb here	3
☐ Personally known by the Notary ☐ ID Type and Number with Issue and Expiration Date ☐ Credible Witness		$	x	Top of thumb here	4
☐ Personally known by the Notary ☐ ID Type and Number with Issue and Expiration Date ☐ Credible Witness		$	x	Top of thumb here	5
☐ Personally known by the Notary ☐ ID Type and Number with Issue and Expiration Date ☐ Credible Witness		$	x	Top of thumb here	6
☐ Personally known by the Notary ☐ ID Type and Number with Issue and Expiration Date ☐ Credible Witness		$	x	Top of thumb here	7
☐ Personally known by the Notary ☐ ID Type and Number with Issue and Expiration Date ☐ Credible Witness		$	x	Top of thumb here	8

1	Date and Time of Notarization	Type of Notarization	Address Where Notarization Performed	Document Type and Date	Name And Address of Signer
1				Date of Document:	
2				Date of Document:	
3				Date of Document:	
4				Date of Document:	
5				Date of Document:	
6				Date of Document:	
7				Date of Document:	
8				Date of Document:	

Identification of Signer	Additional Information	Notary Fee	Signature of Signer	Right Thumbprint of Signer	2
☐ Personally known by the Notary ☐ ID Type and Number with Issue and Expiration Date ☐ Credible Witness		$	x	Top of thumb here	1
☐ Personally known by the Notary ☐ ID Type and Number with Issue and Expiration Date ☐ Credible Witness		$	x	Top of thumb here	2
☐ Personally known by the Notary ☐ ID Type and Number with Issue and Expiration Date ☐ Credible Witness		$	x	Top of thumb here	3
☐ Personally known by the Notary ☐ ID Type and Number with Issue and Expiration Date ☐ Credible Witness		$	x	Top of thumb here	4
☐ Personally known by the Notary ☐ ID Type and Number with Issue and Expiration Date ☐ Credible Witness		$	x	Top of thumb here	5
☐ Personally known by the Notary ☐ ID Type and Number with Issue and Expiration Date ☐ Credible Witness		$	x	Top of thumb here	6
☐ Personally known by the Notary ☐ ID Type and Number with Issue and Expiration Date ☐ Credible Witness		$	x	Top of thumb here	7
☐ Personally known by the Notary ☐ ID Type and Number with Issue and Expiration Date ☐ Credible Witness		$	x	Top of thumb here	8

1	Date and Time of Notarization	Type of Notarization	Address Where Notarization Performed	Document Type and Date	Name And Address of Signer
1				Date of Document:	
2				Date of Document:	
3				Date of Document:	
4				Date of Document:	
5				Date of Document:	
6				Date of Document:	
7				Date of Document:	
8				Date of Document:	

Identification of Signer	Additional Information	Notary Fee	Signature of Signer	Right Thumbprint of Signer	2
☐ Personally known by the Notary ☐ ID Type and Number with Issue and Expiration Date ☐ Credible Witness		$	x	Top of thumb here	1
☐ Personally known by the Notary ☐ ID Type and Number with Issue and Expiration Date ☐ Credible Witness		$	x	Top of thumb here	2
☐ Personally known by the Notary ☐ ID Type and Number with Issue and Expiration Date ☐ Credible Witness		$	x	Top of thumb here	3
☐ Personally known by the Notary ☐ ID Type and Number with Issue and Expiration Date ☐ Credible Witness		$	x	Top of thumb here	4
☐ Personally known by the Notary ☐ ID Type and Number with Issue and Expiration Date ☐ Credible Witness		$	x	Top of thumb here	5
☐ Personally known by the Notary ☐ ID Type and Number with Issue and Expiration Date ☐ Credible Witness		$	x	Top of thumb here	6
☐ Personally known by the Notary ☐ ID Type and Number with Issue and Expiration Date ☐ Credible Witness		$	x	Top of thumb here	7
☐ Personally known by the Notary ☐ ID Type and Number with Issue and Expiration Date ☐ Credible Witness		$	x	Top of thumb here	8

1	Date and Time of Notarization	Type of Notarization	Address Where Notarization Performed	Document Type and Date	Name And Address of Signer
1				Date of Document:	
2				Date of Document:	
3				Date of Document:	
4				Date of Document:	
5				Date of Document:	
6				Date of Document:	
7				Date of Document:	
8				Date of Document:	

Identification of Signer	Additional Information	Notary Fee	Signature of Signer	Right Thumbprint of Signer	2
☐ Personally known by the Notary ☐ ID Type and Number with Issue and Expiration Date ☐ Credible Witness		$	x	Top of thumb here	1
☐ Personally known by the Notary ☐ ID Type and Number with Issue and Expiration Date ☐ Credible Witness		$	x	Top of thumb here	2
☐ Personally known by the Notary ☐ ID Type and Number with Issue and Expiration Date ☐ Credible Witness		$	x	Top of thumb here	3
☐ Personally known by the Notary ☐ ID Type and Number with Issue and Expiration Date ☐ Credible Witness		$	x	Top of thumb here	4
☐ Personally known by the Notary ☐ ID Type and Number with Issue and Expiration Date ☐ Credible Witness		$	x	Top of thumb here	5
☐ Personally known by the Notary ☐ ID Type and Number with Issue and Expiration Date ☐ Credible Witness		$	x	Top of thumb here	6
☐ Personally known by the Notary ☐ ID Type and Number with Issue and Expiration Date ☐ Credible Witness		$	x	Top of thumb here	7
☐ Personally known by the Notary ☐ ID Type and Number with Issue and Expiration Date ☐ Credible Witness		$	x	Top of thumb here	8

1	Date and Time of Notarization	Type of Notarization	Address Where Notarization Performed	Document Type and Date	Name And Address of Signer
1				Date of Document:	
2				Date of Document:	
3				Date of Document:	
4				Date of Document:	
5				Date of Document:	
6				Date of Document:	
7				Date of Document:	
8				Date of Document:	

Identification of Signer	Additional Information	Notary Fee	Signature of Signer	Right Thumbprint of Signer	2
☐ Personally known by the Notary ☐ ID Type and Number with Issue and Expiration Date ☐ Credible Witness		$	x	Top of thumb here	1
☐ Personally known by the Notary ☐ ID Type and Number with Issue and Expiration Date ☐ Credible Witness		$	x	Top of thumb here	2
☐ Personally known by the Notary ☐ ID Type and Number with Issue and Expiration Date ☐ Credible Witness		$	x	Top of thumb here	3
☐ Personally known by the Notary ☐ ID Type and Number with Issue and Expiration Date ☐ Credible Witness		$	x	Top of thumb here	4
☐ Personally known by the Notary ☐ ID Type and Number with Issue and Expiration Date ☐ Credible Witness		$	x	Top of thumb here	5
☐ Personally known by the Notary ☐ ID Type and Number with Issue and Expiration Date ☐ Credible Witness		$	x	Top of thumb here	6
☐ Personally known by the Notary ☐ ID Type and Number with Issue and Expiration Date ☐ Credible Witness		$	x	Top of thumb here	7
☐ Personally known by the Notary ☐ ID Type and Number with Issue and Expiration Date ☐ Credible Witness		$	x	Top of thumb here	8

1	Date and Time of Notarization	Type of Notarization	Address Where Notarization Performed	Document Type and Date	Name And Address of Signer
1				Date of Document:	
2				Date of Document:	
3				Date of Document:	
4				Date of Document:	
5				Date of Document:	
6				Date of Document:	
7				Date of Document:	
8				Date of Document:	

Identification of Signer	Additional Information	Notary Fee	Signature of Signer	Right Thumbprint of Signer	2
☐ Personally known by the Notary ☐ ID Type and Number with Issue and Expiration Date ☐ Credible Witness		$	x	Top of thumb here	1
☐ Personally known by the Notary ☐ ID Type and Number with Issue and Expiration Date ☐ Credible Witness		$	x	Top of thumb here	2
☐ Personally known by the Notary ☐ ID Type and Number with Issue and Expiration Date ☐ Credible Witness		$	x	Top of thumb here	3
☐ Personally known by the Notary ☐ ID Type and Number with Issue and Expiration Date ☐ Credible Witness		$	x	Top of thumb here	4
☐ Personally known by the Notary ☐ ID Type and Number with Issue and Expiration Date ☐ Credible Witness		$	x	Top of thumb here	5
☐ Personally known by the Notary ☐ ID Type and Number with Issue and Expiration Date ☐ Credible Witness		$	x	Top of thumb here	6
☐ Personally known by the Notary ☐ ID Type and Number with Issue and Expiration Date ☐ Credible Witness		$	x	Top of thumb here	7
☐ Personally known by the Notary ☐ ID Type and Number with Issue and Expiration Date ☐ Credible Witness		$	x	Top of thumb here	8

1	Date and Time of Notarization	Type of Notarization	Address Where Notarization Performed	Document Type and Date	Name And Address of Signer
1				Date of Document:	
2				Date of Document:	
3				Date of Document:	
4				Date of Document:	
5				Date of Document:	
6				Date of Document:	
7				Date of Document:	
8				Date of Document:	

Identification of Signer	Additional Information	Notary Fee	Signature of Signer	Right Thumbprint of Signer	2
☐ Personally known by the Notary ☐ ID Type and Number with Issue and Expiration Date ☐ Credible Witness		$	x	Top of thumb here	1
☐ Personally known by the Notary ☐ ID Type and Number with Issue and Expiration Date ☐ Credible Witness		$	x	Top of thumb here	2
☐ Personally known by the Notary ☐ ID Type and Number with Issue and Expiration Date ☐ Credible Witness		$	x	Top of thumb here	3
☐ Personally known by the Notary ☐ ID Type and Number with Issue and Expiration Date ☐ Credible Witness		$	x	Top of thumb here	4
☐ Personally known by the Notary ☐ ID Type and Number with Issue and Expiration Date ☐ Credible Witness		$	x	Top of thumb here	5
☐ Personally known by the Notary ☐ ID Type and Number with Issue and Expiration Date ☐ Credible Witness		$	x	Top of thumb here	6
☐ Personally known by the Notary ☐ ID Type and Number with Issue and Expiration Date ☐ Credible Witness		$	x	Top of thumb here	7
☐ Personally known by the Notary ☐ ID Type and Number with Issue and Expiration Date ☐ Credible Witness		$	x	Top of thumb here	8

1	Date and Time of Notarization	Type of Notarization	Address Where Notarization Performed	Document Type and Date	Name And Address of Signer
1				Date of Document:	
2				Date of Document:	
3				Date of Document:	
4				Date of Document:	
5				Date of Document:	
6				Date of Document:	
7				Date of Document:	
8				Date of Document:	

Identification of Signer	Additional Information	Notary Fee	Signature of Signer	Right Thumbprint of Signer	2
☐ Personally known by the Notary ☐ ID Type and Number with Issue and Expiration Date ☐ Credible Witness		$	x	Top of thumb here	1
☐ Personally known by the Notary ☐ ID Type and Number with Issue and Expiration Date ☐ Credible Witness		$	x	Top of thumb here	2
☐ Personally known by the Notary ☐ ID Type and Number with Issue and Expiration Date ☐ Credible Witness		$	x	Top of thumb here	3
☐ Personally known by the Notary ☐ ID Type and Number with Issue and Expiration Date ☐ Credible Witness		$	x	Top of thumb here	4
☐ Personally known by the Notary ☐ ID Type and Number with Issue and Expiration Date ☐ Credible Witness		$	x	Top of thumb here	5
☐ Personally known by the Notary ☐ ID Type and Number with Issue and Expiration Date ☐ Credible Witness		$	x	Top of thumb here	6
☐ Personally known by the Notary ☐ ID Type and Number with Issue and Expiration Date ☐ Credible Witness		$	x	Top of thumb here	7
☐ Personally known by the Notary ☐ ID Type and Number with Issue and Expiration Date ☐ Credible Witness		$	x	Top of thumb here	8

1	Date and Time of Notarization	Type of Notarization	Address Where Notarization Performed	Document Type and Date	Name And Address of Signer
1				Date of Document:	
2				Date of Document:	
3				Date of Document:	
4				Date of Document:	
5				Date of Document:	
6				Date of Document:	
7				Date of Document:	
8				Date of Document:	

Identification of Signer	Additional Information	Notary Fee	Signature of Signer	Right Thumbprint of Signer	2
☐ Personally known by the Notary ☐ ID Type and Number with Issue and Expiration Date ☐ Credible Witness		$	x	Top of thumb here	1
☐ Personally known by the Notary ☐ ID Type and Number with Issue and Expiration Date ☐ Credible Witness		$	x	Top of thumb here	2
☐ Personally known by the Notary ☐ ID Type and Number with Issue and Expiration Date ☐ Credible Witness		$	x	Top of thumb here	3
☐ Personally known by the Notary ☐ ID Type and Number with Issue and Expiration Date ☐ Credible Witness		$	x	Top of thumb here	4
☐ Personally known by the Notary ☐ ID Type and Number with Issue and Expiration Date ☐ Credible Witness		$	x	Top of thumb here	5
☐ Personally known by the Notary ☐ ID Type and Number with Issue and Expiration Date ☐ Credible Witness		$	x	Top of thumb here	6
☐ Personally known by the Notary ☐ ID Type and Number with Issue and Expiration Date ☐ Credible Witness		$	x	Top of thumb here	7
☐ Personally known by the Notary ☐ ID Type and Number with Issue and Expiration Date ☐ Credible Witness		$	x	Top of thumb here	8

1	Date and Time of Notarization	Type of Notarization	Address Where Notarization Performed	Document Type and Date	Name And Address of Signer
1				Date of Document:	
2				Date of Document:	
3				Date of Document:	
4				Date of Document:	
5				Date of Document:	
6				Date of Document:	
7				Date of Document:	
8				Date of Document:	

Identification of Signer	Additional Information	Notary Fee	Signature of Signer	Right Thumbprint of Signer	2
☐ Personally known by the Notary ☐ ID Type and Number with Issue and Expiration Date ☐ Credible Witness		$	x	Top of thumb here	1
☐ Personally known by the Notary ☐ ID Type and Number with Issue and Expiration Date ☐ Credible Witness		$	x	Top of thumb here	2
☐ Personally known by the Notary ☐ ID Type and Number with Issue and Expiration Date ☐ Credible Witness		$	x	Top of thumb here	3
☐ Personally known by the Notary ☐ ID Type and Number with Issue and Expiration Date ☐ Credible Witness		$	x	Top of thumb here	4
☐ Personally known by the Notary ☐ ID Type and Number with Issue and Expiration Date ☐ Credible Witness		$	x	Top of thumb here	5
☐ Personally known by the Notary ☐ ID Type and Number with Issue and Expiration Date ☐ Credible Witness		$	x	Top of thumb here	6
☐ Personally known by the Notary ☐ ID Type and Number with Issue and Expiration Date ☐ Credible Witness		$	x	Top of thumb here	7
☐ Personally known by the Notary ☐ ID Type and Number with Issue and Expiration Date ☐ Credible Witness		$	x	Top of thumb here	8

1	Date and Time of Notarization	Type of Notarization	Address Where Notarization Performed	Document Type and Date	Name And Address of Signer
1				Date of Document:	
2				Date of Document:	
3				Date of Document:	
4				Date of Document:	
5				Date of Document:	
6				Date of Document:	
7				Date of Document:	
8				Date of Document:	

Identification of Signer	Additional Information	Notary Fee	Signature of Signer	Right Thumbprint of Signer	2
☐ Personally known by the Notary ☐ ID Type and Number with Issue and Expiration Date ☐ Credible Witness		$	x	Top of thumb here	1
☐ Personally known by the Notary ☐ ID Type and Number with Issue and Expiration Date ☐ Credible Witness		$	x	Top of thumb here	2
☐ Personally known by the Notary ☐ ID Type and Number with Issue and Expiration Date ☐ Credible Witness		$	x	Top of thumb here	3
☐ Personally known by the Notary ☐ ID Type and Number with Issue and Expiration Date ☐ Credible Witness		$	x	Top of thumb here	4
☐ Personally known by the Notary ☐ ID Type and Number with Issue and Expiration Date ☐ Credible Witness		$	x	Top of thumb here	5
☐ Personally known by the Notary ☐ ID Type and Number with Issue and Expiration Date ☐ Credible Witness		$	x	Top of thumb here	6
☐ Personally known by the Notary ☐ ID Type and Number with Issue and Expiration Date ☐ Credible Witness		$	x	Top of thumb here	7
☐ Personally known by the Notary ☐ ID Type and Number with Issue and Expiration Date ☐ Credible Witness		$	x	Top of thumb here	8

1	Date and Time of Notarization	Type of Notarization	Address Where Notarization Performed	Document Type and Date	Name And Address of Signer
1				Date of Document:	
2				Date of Document:	
3				Date of Document:	
4				Date of Document:	
5				Date of Document:	
6				Date of Document:	
7				Date of Document:	
8				Date of Document:	

Identification of Signer	Additional Information	Notary Fee	Signature of Signer	Right Thumbprint of Signer	2
☐ Personally known by the Notary ☐ ID Type and Number with Issue and Expiration Date ☐ Credible Witness		$	x	Top of thumb here	1
☐ Personally known by the Notary ☐ ID Type and Number with Issue and Expiration Date ☐ Credible Witness		$	x	Top of thumb here	2
☐ Personally known by the Notary ☐ ID Type and Number with Issue and Expiration Date ☐ Credible Witness		$	x	Top of thumb here	3
☐ Personally known by the Notary ☐ ID Type and Number with Issue and Expiration Date ☐ Credible Witness		$	x	Top of thumb here	4
☐ Personally known by the Notary ☐ ID Type and Number with Issue and Expiration Date ☐ Credible Witness		$	x	Top of thumb here	5
☐ Personally known by the Notary ☐ ID Type and Number with Issue and Expiration Date ☐ Credible Witness		$	x	Top of thumb here	6
☐ Personally known by the Notary ☐ ID Type and Number with Issue and Expiration Date ☐ Credible Witness		$	x	Top of thumb here	7
☐ Personally known by the Notary ☐ ID Type and Number with Issue and Expiration Date ☐ Credible Witness		$	x	Top of thumb here	8

1	Date and Time of Notarization	Type of Notarization	Address Where Notarization Performed	Document Type and Date	Name And Address of Signer
1				Date of Document:	
2				Date of Document:	
3				Date of Document:	
4				Date of Document:	
5				Date of Document:	
6				Date of Document:	
7				Date of Document:	
8				Date of Document:	

Identification of Signer	Additional Information	Notary Fee	Signature of Signer	Right Thumbprint of Signer	2
☐ Personally known by the Notary ☐ ID Type and Number with Issue and Expiration Date ☐ Credible Witness		$	x	Top of thumb here	1
☐ Personally known by the Notary ☐ ID Type and Number with Issue and Expiration Date ☐ Credible Witness		$	x	Top of thumb here	2
☐ Personally known by the Notary ☐ ID Type and Number with Issue and Expiration Date ☐ Credible Witness		$	x	Top of thumb here	3
☐ Personally known by the Notary ☐ ID Type and Number with Issue and Expiration Date ☐ Credible Witness		$	x	Top of thumb here	4
☐ Personally known by the Notary ☐ ID Type and Number with Issue and Expiration Date ☐ Credible Witness		$	x	Top of thumb here	5
☐ Personally known by the Notary ☐ ID Type and Number with Issue and Expiration Date ☐ Credible Witness		$	x	Top of thumb here	6
☐ Personally known by the Notary ☐ ID Type and Number with Issue and Expiration Date ☐ Credible Witness		$	x	Top of thumb here	7
☐ Personally known by the Notary ☐ ID Type and Number with Issue and Expiration Date ☐ Credible Witness		$	x	Top of thumb here	8

1	Date and Time of Notarization	Type of Notarization	Address Where Notarization Performed	Document Type and Date	Name And Address of Signer
1				Date of Document:	
2				Date of Document:	
3				Date of Document:	
4				Date of Document:	
5				Date of Document:	
6				Date of Document:	
7				Date of Document:	
8				Date of Document:	

Identification of Signer	Additional Information	Notary Fee	Signature of Signer	Right Thumbprint of Signer	2
☐ Personally known by the Notary ☐ ID Type and Number with Issue and Expiration Date ☐ Credible Witness		$	x	Top of thumb here	1
☐ Personally known by the Notary ☐ ID Type and Number with Issue and Expiration Date ☐ Credible Witness		$	x	Top of thumb here	2
☐ Personally known by the Notary ☐ ID Type and Number with Issue and Expiration Date ☐ Credible Witness		$	x	Top of thumb here	3
☐ Personally known by the Notary ☐ ID Type and Number with Issue and Expiration Date ☐ Credible Witness		$	x	Top of thumb here	4
☐ Personally known by the Notary ☐ ID Type and Number with Issue and Expiration Date ☐ Credible Witness		$	x	Top of thumb here	5
☐ Personally known by the Notary ☐ ID Type and Number with Issue and Expiration Date ☐ Credible Witness		$	x	Top of thumb here	6
☐ Personally known by the Notary ☐ ID Type and Number with Issue and Expiration Date ☐ Credible Witness		$	x	Top of thumb here	7
☐ Personally known by the Notary ☐ ID Type and Number with Issue and Expiration Date ☐ Credible Witness		$	x	Top of thumb here	8

1	Date and Time of Notarization	Type of Notarization	Address Where Notarization Performed	Document Type and Date	Name And Address of Signer
1				Date of Document:	
2				Date of Document:	
3				Date of Document:	
4				Date of Document:	
5				Date of Document:	
6				Date of Document:	
7				Date of Document:	
8				Date of Document:	

Identification of Signer	Additional Information	Notary Fee	Signature of Signer	Right Thumbprint of Signer	2
☐ Personally known by the Notary ☐ ID Type and Number with Issue and Expiration Date ☐ Credible Witness		$	x	Top of thumb here	1
☐ Personally known by the Notary ☐ ID Type and Number with Issue and Expiration Date ☐ Credible Witness		$	x	Top of thumb here	2
☐ Personally known by the Notary ☐ ID Type and Number with Issue and Expiration Date ☐ Credible Witness		$	x	Top of thumb here	3
☐ Personally known by the Notary ☐ ID Type and Number with Issue and Expiration Date ☐ Credible Witness		$	x	Top of thumb here	4
☐ Personally known by the Notary ☐ ID Type and Number with Issue and Expiration Date ☐ Credible Witness		$	x	Top of thumb here	5
☐ Personally known by the Notary ☐ ID Type and Number with Issue and Expiration Date ☐ Credible Witness		$	x	Top of thumb here	6
☐ Personally known by the Notary ☐ ID Type and Number with Issue and Expiration Date ☐ Credible Witness		$	x	Top of thumb here	7
☐ Personally known by the Notary ☐ ID Type and Number with Issue and Expiration Date ☐ Credible Witness		$	x	Top of thumb here	8

1	Date and Time of Notarization	Type of Notarization	Address Where Notarization Performed	Document Type and Date	Name And Address of Signer
1				Date of Document:	
2				Date of Document:	
3				Date of Document:	
4				Date of Document:	
5				Date of Document:	
6				Date of Document:	
7				Date of Document:	
8				Date of Document:	

Identification of Signer	Additional Information	Notary Fee	Signature of Signer	Right Thumbprint of Signer	2
☐ Personally known by the Notary ☐ ID Type and Number with Issue and Expiration Date ☐ Credible Witness		$	x	Top of thumb here	1
☐ Personally known by the Notary ☐ ID Type and Number with Issue and Expiration Date ☐ Credible Witness		$	x	Top of thumb here	2
☐ Personally known by the Notary ☐ ID Type and Number with Issue and Expiration Date ☐ Credible Witness		$	x	Top of thumb here	3
☐ Personally known by the Notary ☐ ID Type and Number with Issue and Expiration Date ☐ Credible Witness		$	x	Top of thumb here	4
☐ Personally known by the Notary ☐ ID Type and Number with Issue and Expiration Date ☐ Credible Witness		$	x	Top of thumb here	5
☐ Personally known by the Notary ☐ ID Type and Number with Issue and Expiration Date ☐ Credible Witness		$	x	Top of thumb here	6
☐ Personally known by the Notary ☐ ID Type and Number with Issue and Expiration Date ☐ Credible Witness		$	x	Top of thumb here	7
☐ Personally known by the Notary ☐ ID Type and Number with Issue and Expiration Date ☐ Credible Witness		$	x	Top of thumb here	8

1	Date and Time of Notarization	Type of Notarization	Address Where Notarization Performed	Document Type and Date	Name And Address of Signer
1				Date of Document:	
2				Date of Document:	
3				Date of Document:	
4				Date of Document:	
5				Date of Document:	
6				Date of Document:	
7				Date of Document:	
8				Date of Document:	

Identification of Signer	Additional Information	Notary Fee	Signature of Signer	Right Thumbprint of Signer	2
☐ Personally known by the Notary ☐ ID Type and Number with Issue and Expiration Date ☐ Credible Witness		$	x	Top of thumb here	1
☐ Personally known by the Notary ☐ ID Type and Number with Issue and Expiration Date ☐ Credible Witness		$	x	Top of thumb here	2
☐ Personally known by the Notary ☐ ID Type and Number with Issue and Expiration Date ☐ Credible Witness		$	x	Top of thumb here	3
☐ Personally known by the Notary ☐ ID Type and Number with Issue and Expiration Date ☐ Credible Witness		$	x	Top of thumb here	4
☐ Personally known by the Notary ☐ ID Type and Number with Issue and Expiration Date ☐ Credible Witness		$	x	Top of thumb here	5
☐ Personally known by the Notary ☐ ID Type and Number with Issue and Expiration Date ☐ Credible Witness		$	x	Top of thumb here	6
☐ Personally known by the Notary ☐ ID Type and Number with Issue and Expiration Date ☐ Credible Witness		$	x	Top of thumb here	7
☐ Personally known by the Notary ☐ ID Type and Number with Issue and Expiration Date ☐ Credible Witness		$	x	Top of thumb here	8

1	Date and Time of Notarization	Type of Notarization	Address Where Notarization Performed	Document Type and Date	Name And Address of Signer
1				Date of Document:	
2				Date of Document:	
3				Date of Document:	
4				Date of Document:	
5				Date of Document:	
6				Date of Document:	
7				Date of Document:	
8				Date of Document:	

Identification of Signer	Additional Information	Notary Fee	Signature of Signer	Right Thumbprint of Signer	2
☐ Personally known by the Notary ☐ ID Type and Number with Issue and Expiration Date ☐ Credible Witness		$	x	Top of thumb here	1
☐ Personally known by the Notary ☐ ID Type and Number with Issue and Expiration Date ☐ Credible Witness		$	x	Top of thumb here	2
☐ Personally known by the Notary ☐ ID Type and Number with Issue and Expiration Date ☐ Credible Witness		$	x	Top of thumb here	3
☐ Personally known by the Notary ☐ ID Type and Number with Issue and Expiration Date ☐ Credible Witness		$	x	Top of thumb here	4
☐ Personally known by the Notary ☐ ID Type and Number with Issue and Expiration Date ☐ Credible Witness		$	x	Top of thumb here	5
☐ Personally known by the Notary ☐ ID Type and Number with Issue and Expiration Date ☐ Credible Witness		$	x	Top of thumb here	6
☐ Personally known by the Notary ☐ ID Type and Number with Issue and Expiration Date ☐ Credible Witness		$	x	Top of thumb here	7
☐ Personally known by the Notary ☐ ID Type and Number with Issue and Expiration Date ☐ Credible Witness		$	x	Top of thumb here	8

1	Date and Time of Notarization	Type of Notarization	Address Where Notarization Performed	Document Type and Date	Name And Address of Signer
1				Date of Document:	
2				Date of Document:	
3				Date of Document:	
4				Date of Document:	
5				Date of Document:	
6				Date of Document:	
7				Date of Document:	
8				Date of Document:	

Identification of Signer	Additional Information	Notary Fee	Signature of Signer	Right Thumbprint of Signer	2
☐ Personally known by the Notary ☐ ID Type and Number with Issue and Expiration Date ☐ Credible Witness		$	x	Top of thumb here	1
☐ Personally known by the Notary ☐ ID Type and Number with Issue and Expiration Date ☐ Credible Witness		$	x	Top of thumb here	2
☐ Personally known by the Notary ☐ ID Type and Number with Issue and Expiration Date ☐ Credible Witness		$	x	Top of thumb here	3
☐ Personally known by the Notary ☐ ID Type and Number with Issue and Expiration Date ☐ Credible Witness		$	x	Top of thumb here	4
☐ Personally known by the Notary ☐ ID Type and Number with Issue and Expiration Date ☐ Credible Witness		$	x	Top of thumb here	5
☐ Personally known by the Notary ☐ ID Type and Number with Issue and Expiration Date ☐ Credible Witness		$	x	Top of thumb here	6
☐ Personally known by the Notary ☐ ID Type and Number with Issue and Expiration Date ☐ Credible Witness		$	x	Top of thumb here	7
☐ Personally known by the Notary ☐ ID Type and Number with Issue and Expiration Date ☐ Credible Witness		$	x	Top of thumb here	8

1	Date and Time of Notarization	Type of Notarization	Address Where Notarization Performed	Document Type and Date	Name And Address of Signer
1				Date of Document:	
2				Date of Document:	
3				Date of Document:	
4				Date of Document:	
5				Date of Document:	
6				Date of Document:	
7				Date of Document:	
8				Date of Document:	

Identification of Signer	Additional Information	Notary Fee	Signature of Signer	Right Thumbprint of Signer	2
☐ Personally known by the Notary ☐ ID Type and Number with Issue and Expiration Date ☐ Credible Witness		$	x	Top of thumb here	1
☐ Personally known by the Notary ☐ ID Type and Number with Issue and Expiration Date ☐ Credible Witness		$	x	Top of thumb here	2
☐ Personally known by the Notary ☐ ID Type and Number with Issue and Expiration Date ☐ Credible Witness		$	x	Top of thumb here	3
☐ Personally known by the Notary ☐ ID Type and Number with Issue and Expiration Date ☐ Credible Witness		$	x	Top of thumb here	4
☐ Personally known by the Notary ☐ ID Type and Number with Issue and Expiration Date ☐ Credible Witness		$	x	Top of thumb here	5
☐ Personally known by the Notary ☐ ID Type and Number with Issue and Expiration Date ☐ Credible Witness		$	x	Top of thumb here	6
☐ Personally known by the Notary ☐ ID Type and Number with Issue and Expiration Date ☐ Credible Witness		$	x	Top of thumb here	7
☐ Personally known by the Notary ☐ ID Type and Number with Issue and Expiration Date ☐ Credible Witness		$	x	Top of thumb here	8

1	Date and Time of Notarization	Type of Notarization	Address Where Notarization Performed	Document Type and Date	Name And Address of Signer
1				Date of Document:	
2				Date of Document:	
3				Date of Document:	
4				Date of Document:	
5				Date of Document:	
6				Date of Document:	
7				Date of Document:	
8				Date of Document:	

Identification of Signer	Additional Information	Notary Fee	Signature of Signer	Right Thumbprint of Signer	2
☐ Personally known by the Notary ☐ ID Type and Number with Issue and Expiration Date ☐ Credible Witness		$	x	Top of thumb here	1
☐ Personally known by the Notary ☐ ID Type and Number with Issue and Expiration Date ☐ Credible Witness		$	x	Top of thumb here	2
☐ Personally known by the Notary ☐ ID Type and Number with Issue and Expiration Date ☐ Credible Witness		$	x	Top of thumb here	3
☐ Personally known by the Notary ☐ ID Type and Number with Issue and Expiration Date ☐ Credible Witness		$	x	Top of thumb here	4
☐ Personally known by the Notary ☐ ID Type and Number with Issue and Expiration Date ☐ Credible Witness		$	x	Top of thumb here	5
☐ Personally known by the Notary ☐ ID Type and Number with Issue and Expiration Date ☐ Credible Witness		$	x	Top of thumb here	6
☐ Personally known by the Notary ☐ ID Type and Number with Issue and Expiration Date ☐ Credible Witness		$	x	Top of thumb here	7
☐ Personally known by the Notary ☐ ID Type and Number with Issue and Expiration Date ☐ Credible Witness		$	x	Top of thumb here	8

1	Date and Time of Notarization	Type of Notarization	Address Where Notarization Performed	Document Type and Date	Name And Address of Signer
1				Date of Document:	
2				Date of Document:	
3				Date of Document:	
4				Date of Document:	
5				Date of Document:	
6				Date of Document:	
7				Date of Document:	
8				Date of Document:	

Identification of Signer	Additional Information	Notary Fee	Signature of Signer	Right Thumbprint of Signer	2
☐ Personally known by the Notary ☐ ID Type and Number with Issue and Expiration Date ☐ Credible Witness		$	x	Top of thumb here	1
☐ Personally known by the Notary ☐ ID Type and Number with Issue and Expiration Date ☐ Credible Witness		$	x	Top of thumb here	2
☐ Personally known by the Notary ☐ ID Type and Number with Issue and Expiration Date ☐ Credible Witness		$	x	Top of thumb here	3
☐ Personally known by the Notary ☐ ID Type and Number with Issue and Expiration Date ☐ Credible Witness		$	x	Top of thumb here	4
☐ Personally known by the Notary ☐ ID Type and Number with Issue and Expiration Date ☐ Credible Witness		$	x	Top of thumb here	5
☐ Personally known by the Notary ☐ ID Type and Number with Issue and Expiration Date ☐ Credible Witness		$	x	Top of thumb here	6
☐ Personally known by the Notary ☐ ID Type and Number with Issue and Expiration Date ☐ Credible Witness		$	x	Top of thumb here	7
☐ Personally known by the Notary ☐ ID Type and Number with Issue and Expiration Date ☐ Credible Witness		$	x	Top of thumb here	8

1	Date and Time of Notarization	Type of Notarization	Address Where Notarization Performed	Document Type and Date	Name And Address of Signer
1				Date of Document:	
2				Date of Document:	
3				Date of Document:	
4				Date of Document:	
5				Date of Document:	
6				Date of Document:	
7				Date of Document:	
8				Date of Document:	

Identification of Signer	Additional Information	Notary Fee	Signature of Signer	Right Thumbprint of Signer	2
☐ Personally known by the Notary ☐ ID Type and Number with Issue and Expiration Date ☐ Credible Witness		$	x	Top of thumb here	1
☐ Personally known by the Notary ☐ ID Type and Number with Issue and Expiration Date ☐ Credible Witness		$	x	Top of thumb here	2
☐ Personally known by the Notary ☐ ID Type and Number with Issue and Expiration Date ☐ Credible Witness		$	x	Top of thumb here	3
☐ Personally known by the Notary ☐ ID Type and Number with Issue and Expiration Date ☐ Credible Witness		$	x	Top of thumb here	4
☐ Personally known by the Notary ☐ ID Type and Number with Issue and Expiration Date ☐ Credible Witness		$	x	Top of thumb here	5
☐ Personally known by the Notary ☐ ID Type and Number with Issue and Expiration Date ☐ Credible Witness		$	x	Top of thumb here	6
☐ Personally known by the Notary ☐ ID Type and Number with Issue and Expiration Date ☐ Credible Witness		$	x	Top of thumb here	7
☐ Personally known by the Notary ☐ ID Type and Number with Issue and Expiration Date ☐ Credible Witness		$	x	Top of thumb here	8

1	Date and Time of Notarization	Type of Notarization	Address Where Notarization Performed	Document Type and Date	Name And Address of Signer
1				Date of Document:	
2				Date of Document:	
3				Date of Document:	
4				Date of Document:	
5				Date of Document:	
6				Date of Document:	
7				Date of Document:	
8				Date of Document:	

Identification of Signer	Additional Information	Notary Fee	Signature of Signer	Right Thumbprint of Signer	2
☐ Personally known by the Notary ☐ ID Type and Number with Issue and Expiration Date ☐ Credible Witness		$	x	Top of thumb here	1
☐ Personally known by the Notary ☐ ID Type and Number with Issue and Expiration Date ☐ Credible Witness		$	x	Top of thumb here	2
☐ Personally known by the Notary ☐ ID Type and Number with Issue and Expiration Date ☐ Credible Witness		$	x	Top of thumb here	3
☐ Personally known by the Notary ☐ ID Type and Number with Issue and Expiration Date ☐ Credible Witness		$	x	Top of thumb here	4
☐ Personally known by the Notary ☐ ID Type and Number with Issue and Expiration Date ☐ Credible Witness		$	x	Top of thumb here	5
☐ Personally known by the Notary ☐ ID Type and Number with Issue and Expiration Date ☐ Credible Witness		$	x	Top of thumb here	6
☐ Personally known by the Notary ☐ ID Type and Number with Issue and Expiration Date ☐ Credible Witness		$	x	Top of thumb here	7
☐ Personally known by the Notary ☐ ID Type and Number with Issue and Expiration Date ☐ Credible Witness		$	x	Top of thumb here	8

1	Date and Time of Notarization	Type of Notarization	Address Where Notarization Performed	Document Type and Date	Name And Address of Signer
1				Date of Document:	
2				Date of Document:	
3				Date of Document:	
4				Date of Document:	
5				Date of Document:	
6				Date of Document:	
7				Date of Document:	
8				Date of Document:	

Identification of Signer	Additional Information	Notary Fee	Signature of Signer	Right Thumbprint of Signer	2
☐ Personally known by the Notary ☐ ID Type and Number with Issue and Expiration Date ☐ Credible Witness		$	x	Top of thumb here	1
☐ Personally known by the Notary ☐ ID Type and Number with Issue and Expiration Date ☐ Credible Witness		$	x	Top of thumb here	2
☐ Personally known by the Notary ☐ ID Type and Number with Issue and Expiration Date ☐ Credible Witness		$	x	Top of thumb here	3
☐ Personally known by the Notary ☐ ID Type and Number with Issue and Expiration Date ☐ Credible Witness		$	x	Top of thumb here	4
☐ Personally known by the Notary ☐ ID Type and Number with Issue and Expiration Date ☐ Credible Witness		$	x	Top of thumb here	5
☐ Personally known by the Notary ☐ ID Type and Number with Issue and Expiration Date ☐ Credible Witness		$	x	Top of thumb here	6
☐ Personally known by the Notary ☐ ID Type and Number with Issue and Expiration Date ☐ Credible Witness		$	x	Top of thumb here	7
☐ Personally known by the Notary ☐ ID Type and Number with Issue and Expiration Date ☐ Credible Witness		$	x	Top of thumb here	8

www.ingramcontent.com/pod-product-compliance
Lightning Source LLC
LaVergne TN
LVHW070819210926
848482LV00005B/291
9798295519826